NEOORTHODOXY

By

CHARLES CALDWELL RYRIE

MOODY PRESS • CHICAGO

This Book Is Gratefully Dedicated to
Mr. and Mrs. William C. Muir
Mr. and Mrs. Frank E. Balfour
Mr. and Mrs. John Black
whose Christian love and kindness were without limit
during my stay in their city of
Edinburgh, Scotland

CONTENTS

1

Why This Book?

IT HAS BEEN approximately fifty years since neoortho-doxy was born into this world through the writings of Karl Barth. Since then it has not only spread rapidly but has traveled in the best circles. Today it is being taught in scores of seminaries and preached from many church pulpits which a few years ago were considered fundamental. Too, neoorthodoxy has developed a prolific and peculiarly deceptive body of literature to help propagate its beliefs.

Exactly what is neoorthodoxy and how does it affect those who subscribe to its strange and hard-to-understand tenets? Is it merely a question for theological debate or does it reach the level of the man in the pew? How can it be recognized? Should we be grateful to Barthianism for delivering the church from the curse of the old liberalism or is neoorthodoxy part of the increasing spirit of Antichrist in Christendom? To seek an answer to these and other questions is the purpose of this book.

Barthianism with its call to the Word of God has excited a lot of preachers and theologians in the last several decades. The only trouble with it is, if one studies it, he soon discovers that the call is to the *faith* of the

Word and not to the *facts* of the Bible which are actually, to Barthianism, of secondary importance. And yet the difficulty is that too few conservative pastors and laymen have been able to study something concise, nontechnical, but accurate on this subject. To help meet this need is the purpose of this book.

Barthianism, we recognize, is a term deplored by Barth himself, but it has come to stand for a theological viewpoint in which Barth was and is one of the leading voices. It has been hailed as the new or neoorthodoxy; in reality it is nothing but a false or pseudoorthodoxy. How widespread is this system? That is a very difficult question to answer because neoorthodoxy has many varieties. In some European countries and in liberal seminaries in this country, it is only an academic study. In other places it has not only permeated academic circles but has also sifted through to the pulpit. It is unquestionably the theological system taught in some American seminaries which formerly stood for conservative truth. The danger is that since the terminology of Barthianism and conservatism is the same in many areas, the change in these schools and their graduates is not readily discerned. Too many are too quick to whitewash schools and men who still speak of regeneration, inspiration, the authority of the Word, etc., and too few have investigated what is really meant by those terms. The danger of such is like quicksand.

There is another deception in neoorthodoxy, and that is its inconsistency—some good along with the bad. But it is this good which is like a smoke screen to some evangelicals, and there is abroad the feeling that perhaps, after all, Barthianism isn't so bad, and we shouldn't criticize it so harshly because it has done some good. It is true that certain isolated statements sound good, but those statements seen in the context of the system take on an entirely different meaning. To show as simply as possible something of the system and its errors is the purpose of this book.

2

Names, Values, Cautions

IT HAS ALREADY been suggested that Barthianism is a term that Barth himself rejects since he does not consider himself the head of any movement. We can be sympathetic with him in this, but can hardly feel that it is a realistic appraisal of the situation. No doubt Calvin would reject the term *Calvinism* and Arminius *Arminianism,* but when a man takes issue with the current theological thought, and when others follow him in that new stream of thought, he and they can expect themselves to be dubbed with the leader's name. It makes little difference whether or not all follow every detail of the teaching of the leader—the name sticks anyway.

Neoorthodoxy is another name for Barthianism. This name came from the new thought's call back to the Word, the sovereignty of God, the sinfulness of man, and the need of forgiveness. In the midst of the liberalism in which this call came, it did seem like a return to orthodoxy and was naturally hailed as the new orthodoxy. Indeed, many Barthians still claim to stand in the center of the stream of Reformed theology and consider themselves twentieth century Calvinists. The similarities between Barthian and Reformed doctrine are often pointed out by the Barthians. This is one of the reasons why many conservatives have been deceived into thinking that Barthianism is indeed a new orthodoxy.

Theology of Crisis is another name given to this school of thought. The crisis idea developed from the historical situation in which Barthianism was cast. Two world wars had swept the foundation of optimism away from liberal theology, and, as usually happens, the aftermath of the wars saw the breaking of every sacred tie known to man. This the Barthians saw as an act of revolt against God deserving of His wrath, and they intensified their call to man to see himself standing on the very brink of Hell. The crisis could not be more real, and the Theology of Crisis in all genuineness and sincerity calls upon men to realize this and seek forgiveness from God.

Some of the values of being informed about Barthianism should be obvious by now. The system must be something very good or something terribly deceiving, and we must know which. The widespread acceptance of it in many circles, and especially the notion in evangelical circles that maybe there is something good in it, makes it incumbent on us to know exactly what is in it. Too, the similarities of terminology between Barthianism and conservative theology make it imperative to know more of the system than a few isolated phrases. It is not enough to know whether neoorthodoxy teaches that the Bible *is* the Word of God or whether the Bible *becomes* the Word of God. Other doctrines must be reviewed as well as an understanding of what is meant by the terms and phrases used.

Some words of caution are in order. First, we must always remember that our standard of judgment is solely the Word of God. It is not our preconceived notions about the Bible, or necessarily what we have been taught, but what the Bible actually says. We are too prone to try to pour everything into our little mold; if it fits, fine; if not, then it is wrong.

Second, be cautioned against failing to see the system as a whole. There are many limitations inherent in the brevity of a book like this, but an advantage is that one cannot get bogged down in details simply for lack of space. Beware of being deceived by seemingly good statements; always fit them into the whole.

Third, remember that all Barthians do not follow Barth in every detail. Many have been influenced by his writings who obviously do not follow him. In this book we can only deal with a few Barthians, and even in dealing with their teachings, it will be necessary to generalize.

Finally, beware of a blanket condemnation of men. One cannot always determine whether or not these men are Christians. However, that does not mean that their teaching is true nor that we should not criticize it; but to criticize the system is one thing; to have a wrong heart attitude toward men is quite another. "And this I pray, that your love may abound yet more and more in knowledge and all discernment" as you study Barthianism.

3

Personalities

KARL BARTH, the titular head of the neoorthodox school, was born May 10, 1886, in Basel, Switzerland. His father was a lecturer in theology in the university of that city. Barth himself was educated in the universities of Bern, Berlin, Tübingen, and Marburg, and he studied under such distinguished professors as Harnack and Herrmann. He has served as assistant pastor, pastor, and professor in several universities, and lately he has been lecturing and writing in the city of his birth. Highlights of his career include the publication of *The Epistle to the Romans* in 1918 (which fell like a bombshell on the theological world), his forced exit in 1935 from Germany because of his uncompromising opposition to Hitlerism, and his present occupation of writing the massive volumes of *Church Dogmatics*.

Many of Barth's later writings are not available in English; hence it is difficult for the average person to judge his work and thought fairly. However, there are several books in English which serve as good guides to the thought of Barth today. They are Arnold B. Come's *An Introduction to Barth's "Dogmatics" for Preachers* and Barth's own *Evangelical Theology, An Introduction*.

Two excellent, though technical, critiques of Barth are *Karl Barth's Doctrine of Holy Scripture* by Klaas Runia and *Christianity and Barthianism* by Cornelius Van Til.

Emil Brunner is also a Swiss having been born near Zurich, December 23, 1889. He has studied in Zurich, Berlin, and Union Seminary, New York. He too has been an assistant pastor, pastor, and professor. Most of his teaching career has been spent as professor of Systematic and Practical Theology in the University of Zurich. His books are many—*The Mediator, The Theology of Crisis, The Divine Imperative,* and *Man in Revolt* are but a few. These are available to the English reader. Brunner has been along with Barth one of the leading voices in neoorthodoxy though Brunner's voice has been more moderate. Brunner's acceptance of natural theology led to controversy (now largely defunct) with Barth who refused to include natural theology in his system. Of Barth, Brunner writes: "I have been acquainted with Karl Barth—though only slightly— since 1917. I have never been in close relationship with Barth [as is often said]."[1]

The third neoorthodox voice is an American, Reinhold Niebuhr. He was born in Wright City, Missouri, June 21, 1892. He was educated at Elmhurst College, Eden Theological Seminary, and Yale University. He too has been a pastor and professor, which latter position he now holds in Christian Ethics and Philosophy of Religion at Union Theological Seminary, New York. Niebuhr represents a reaction against liberalism which he felt was far too optimistic; yet he retained one aspect of liberal teaching, namely, the social gospel. One may say that he is right wing in his theological position and

---

[1] In a letter to E. L. Allen, *Creation and Grace,* p. 6.

left wing in his social ethics. One of the most decisive influences on this man's life was a personal experience he had while a pastor in Detroit. During his pastorate in the years of rapid expansion in the auto industry, he found himself more and more in sympathy with the average worker of his congregation and his needs. Feeling that even high wages were merely a front for exploitation of the worker for purposes of mass production, the young pastor championed the rising labor movement. He never lost the determination gained in those years to preserve at all costs human and social values, and consequently his theological thinking is always in terms of social and political ethics and their practical implications for our day. His books are many and include *Does Civilization Need Religion?*, *Moral Man and Immoral Society*, *Interpretation of Christian Ethics*, *The Nature and Destiny of Man*, and *The Irony of American History.*

4

Historical and Theological Background

THE STORY STARTS with the Reformation and the Renaissance. Although these two movements were not contemporaneous, they were complementary. One was in the realm of the conscience; the other in the realm of the intellect. One was God-centered; the other, man-centered. One found its source in the Bible; the other, in classical culture. One was evangelicalism; the other, humanism. In time the humanism of the Renaissance gained prominence over the orthodoxy of the Reformation, and reason began to triumph over faith.

The first check to the rationalism and materialism of the Renaissance was the theology of Schleiermacher (1768-1834). He is generally considered the father of modern liberalism, for he found his authority, not in the Scriptures, but in the soul's experiences. Although he (or anyone else) could not build a theology on such subjectivism, theologians followed his lead for a hundred years, and we are still reaping what he sowed in the present-day substitution of psychology for religion.

Not long after Schleiermacher died, Darwin put forth his evolutionary hypothesis. This is part of the story because of its tremendous effect in undermining the authority of the Scriptures. Indeed, the whole idea of an unchanging authority was blasted by evolution. Related to Darwin and his so-called scientific method was the higher criticism of the nineteenth century. Higher critics sought for the origin of the ideas of the Bible and turned their investigations to the conditions of life which existed at the time of the writing of the Scriptures. Actually, there is a legitimate field for investigation in these areas, but the result of the way the higher critics did it was the invalidating of any kind of belief in an a priori, preexistent norm of truth. Inspiration was redefined in terms of the author instead of the writing. Insofar as the Bible was true it was inspired, but it was the task of the liberal critic to determine at what points the Bible was true. Harnack (1851-1930) and Herrmann (1846-1922) (under whom Barth studied) were leaders in this religious-historical school.

What were the results of this teaching of liberalism? There was a high and false estimation of the ability of human nature. It promoted the illusion that the kingdom of God was capable of being fulfilled in history, for man's ability could bring this to pass. There came with it the abandonment of the distinctive and exclusive character of the message of the Gospel and the loss of the uniqueness of Christianity; and secularization of life and thought can also be traced, at least in part, to the teaching of liberalism in the last century.

But all of this did not go unchallenged. There have been reactions against liberal theology of which neoorthodoxy is one. Before Barth raised his voice in protest, however, other factors were already at work. The humanists in their own way were a reactionary group with their gospel of salvation by scientific research and cooperative effort. Actually, they were only using the principles which the liberals had proposed, but they carried them to their logical extreme. Their faith in man assured the world that society could be provided now with what the modernists were hoping for some day. Actually, the humanists were out-liberalizing the liberals, and this caused the liberals to stop and take stock of their principles.

The tragedy of the first world war played a very large part in shattering the presuppositions of modernism. The golden age seemed very far off then, and human nature that could invent the atrocities of both wars was hardly something to put one's faith in. Men now began to look for authority, and that was something modernism could not provide.

Into this situation came the voice of Karl Barth. He cried against the subjectivism of liberalism—against their concern with emotions and experiences instead of the truth of God. He deplored the surrender to psychology and expressed the crying need for absolute authority. The religious-historical school's investigations into origins had brought about a famine of doctrine, for the Scripture had lost all meaning for men in their own day. It is little wonder that this call back to authoritarianism was hailed as the new orthodoxy. In the darkness of the time in which it came, it was like a light in a blackout. Whether or not Barthianism has succeeded in supplying this authority remains to be seen, but in the historical and theological context, it was like a clarion call sounding against all that was human, beginning with the Renaissance, continuing with Schleiermacher, Darwin, the higher critics, humanism, and culminating in the liberal modernism of that day. It was a call back to things divine. It was a call to let God be God.

Barthianism, then, was a reaction against liberalism,

but has it had any effect on liberals? Unquestionably it has, for liberals have been forced to examine their own premises and in many cases modify them. The modified view is sometimes called today the new or neo-liberalism. Of it, one of its leaders says, "It still asserts the creativeness and potentiality of the human spirit, but it is also much more aware of the limitations of the human spirit—for example, it takes sin seriously. It is not as optimistic as it used to be, but it is not as pessimistic as neoorthodoxy."[1]

Barthianism attempts to be a synthesis between liberalism and conservatism, and no doubt it has succeeded in dulling the sharpness of the liberal antitheses. What has it done to conservatism? In some circles that formerly were conservative, it has taken over, for in embracing neoorthodoxy one can be at the same time a respectable intellectual (by believing evolution and destructive aspects of higher criticism) and an orthodox evangelical (by preaching the Gospel in the usual terms). In some fundamental groups its influence has not been felt or even heard of. In others, one fears sometimes that a little of it has rubbed off, not doctrinally perhaps, but practically; for there is abroad the notion that to be extreme is not respectable, but to promote a synthesis is often desirable. In days when others are promoting a new orthodoxy and a new liberalism, let us beware of promoting any sort of so-called new fundamentalism which by its conciliatory nature tends to dull the keen edge of the distinctiveness, exclusiveness, and aggressiveness of historic Christianity.

---

[1] J. C. Bauer, Dean of the University of Chicago Theological Faculty, *Time,* April 18, 1955.

5

Barth's Developing Theology

K ARL BARTH is not a man to stand still intellectually. His theology is a developing one, and that makes the analysis of it difficult. Reading his work on *Romans* will not give one a complete insight to his thought today. It is not only a question of what he said, but when he said it.

Up to the time of the writing of his commentary on Romans in 1918, Barth was struggling with the influences of his training. Schleiermacher and the Lutheran tradition were two of those influences of his earlier life. He had studied the teachings of liberalism though his own outlook was not that of a thoroughgoing liberal since even at this stage he was acutely aware of the nature of sin as rebellion against God. He had read widely in philosophy, and much of it was crumbling under his searching questions. It was during the time of his first pastorate that a struggle was going on in his soul as to how to reach his people with the Word of God. He began to realize that people come to church, not to hear the opinions of the preacher, but to hear a message from God.

The Epistle to the Romans was a deliberate bombshell designed to explode on the theological world. It succeeded, too, for the book either shattered the liberals or angered them. It had one supreme message—let God be God. Man cannot grasp the Eternal, and even natural theology can only build an altar to the unknown God. But the Eternal can grasp man, and the Cross of Christ is the unique expression of the meeting of God and man.

During the decades, since *Romans* up to the present time of writing the *Church Dogmatics,* there have been other stages of development. There was a state of examining current philosophies as they especially related to the course of history. This was at the time when Hitler was dominating Germany. Then there came an emphasis on the bankruptness of man. Man is actually denatured by sin, and grace must enter the picture if there is to be any hope. The Word of God slays by showing man what he is, and it makes alive by showing the grace of Christ. This led to the stage of dialectical expression. This simply means that the only way to express the whole truth is by making contradictory statements. It is not an affirmative *or* a negative that really expresses the truth, but a yes *and* a no. This was especially prominent in his thinking about time and eternity, or eschatology. Eschatology was seen as the core of faith, and Barthianism is permeated with the eschatological idea of God's breaking through into history.

During all of this time, Barth's theology was becoming more and more the Theology of the Word, not in the sense of propositions, but in the sense of a personal Word. Philosophy finds less place in his system now; it is all the Word. The Word became flesh in the incarnation, but it cannot be stated in doctrinal propositions. From his own viewpoint Barth is biblical because revelation is in Jesus Christ. From our viewpoint he is not at all biblical because he denies the possibility of stating the truths of the Bible in propositions. His present massive work is called *Church Dogmatics* because it is the examination which the *Church* makes with respect to the language about God. The Word is made flesh in the Church just like it was, he says, in the Acts of the Apostles. For all his desire to be objective and authoritarian this would seem to be a very subjective approach —but more of that later. The dialectical expression developed earlier finds wide use in the *Dogmatics*. Barth's method of stating the truth is by using many subordinate clauses. He seems to go round and round until finally he thinks he has confronted you with the truth as a whole. His outlook is certainly much more biblical than it used to be though the Bible still merely attests to revelation—it is not revelation in itself.

What shall we say of this man and his work, not in the light yet of its doctrinal content, but in the light of its place in history? He did something about liberalism that few others have been able to do. *Romans* made itself felt. He made people realize that a theologian should be something other than a historian or philosopher or psychologist. He restored to theology, at a time when it had lost nearly everything, a voice of authority as if from God. He curbed the secularizing trend with his new thought. His theological outlook is avowedly Christian, for he understands the task of theology as the stating of the content and meaning of our faith. He lays great stress on the sovereignty of God and emphasizes supernaturalism. He has a biblical emphasis in that his writings are filled with exegesis of the Sacred Text. Whether we agree with him or not, he must be recognized as one of the greatest theologians of our time, and all who meet him testify to the fact that he is, above all, a Christian gentleman.

He has served in his own lifetime to change the theological climate of the world. He took the chill off liberalism. He is not a fundamentalist, but the presence of neoorthodoxy in the world has made it easier for evangelicals to talk about supernaturalism, the atonement, and even the second coming of Christ. We are glad for what Barthianism has said, not because of what was said *per se,* but because what was said was said at a very critical time in Church history. To be indebted historically is one thing; to be indebted doctrinally, another. Too many are confused at this point. Broadly speaking, the Barthian emphasis was in the right direction, i.e., toward supernaturalism and away from humanism, toward God and away from man—and we are grateful for that; but the specific Barthian content of that emphasis is something with which evangelicals cannot agree. This we must see in the succeeding chapters.

6

Barth's Point of View—Sovereignty

WE HAVE ALREADY NOTED that there are many variations within the neoorthodox group. It may be profitable, then, to look in a general way at the different points of view of Barth, Brunner, and Niebuhr. Then we will be in a better position to summarize neoorthodox teaching on various doctrines.

If it may be summarized in a word, the point of view of Karl Barth is the sovereignty of God. Due to his own experience as a pastor who realized that his people came on Sunday to hear a message from God, the center of his thinking passed from man to God. *Our* ideas about God do not really matter. What does matter is God's Word to us, and this may come, because God is sovereign, in the Bible, or in a sermon, or even in things. Let God be God was in effect the watchword, and because God is God, He never passes over to the human side.

Why God has been pleased to reveal anything at all we cannot know, Barth says; we can only humbly accept the fact that He has and then investigate that revelation. Primarily, God is known in the Word, Jesus Christ, for that is where He has chosen to reveal Himself. Since Jesus Christ is found in the Scriptures, the Bible attests to the Word of God. The Word, that is the sovereign self-communication of God in Christ, reaches us through the intermediary of the Scriptures, and the Scriptures reach us through the mediation of the Church. The authority of the Word (Christ) then is absolute. The authority of the Bible is not quite so absolute, for even though it has authority from God, the authentication of that authority depends on the awakening of faith in us. It is not quite that you and I choose what in the Bible is the Word of God for us, for Barth recognizes that the Church has found the Word in many places in the Bible where an individual has not found it; but there certainly is an element of a subjective standard in his concept of the authority of the Bible. Revelation is not confined to what I think is the Word; yet it does not become the Word until I recognize it as such (and even that recognition is a sovereign act of God). Thus it is possible to say that Barth believes the Bible *is* the Word of God and at the same time say that he believes the Bible *becomes* the Word of God.

But let us go back to Barth's idea about Jesus Christ. In Him God has bridged the gap by entering the world in a man. This is the only way it could be bridged because of the great gulf fixed between sinful man and sovereign God. The significance of Jesus Christ is not in the historical Jesus since it is hard, Barth says, to get information about Him, but the significance is in the Cross. In the Cross we can see the inadequacy of all that is human; in the resurrection (though it doesn't really matter what happened historically at the tomb) humanity was taken up into God and thus the way was opened to God.

The reader will have noticed already that in this conception the facts of the Bible play a very unimportant part. If you believe that John's Gospel, for instance, presents no facts but only pictures of the life of Christ, it really will make no difference to your faith in Christ. It can be true that Christ is the Bread of Life even though Jesus never spoke the discourse recorded in John 6. Likewise, it is not at all necessary to faith to believe in a bodily resurrection of the Lord, for we are supposed to be able to believe in resurrection anyway. One can see from this why Barthianism is called the new orthodoxy because it speaks of the Cross and resurrection in orthodox terms, but it certainly does not attach to these events the orthodox meaning. In reality, then, it is a pseudoorthodoxy. It is impossible and illogical to believe that you can have the faith of the New Testament without the facts.

In fairness it should be added that in recent years Barth's view of the Scriptures has become more conservative, and especially his view of the resurrection. But he still believes that the Bible is only a witness to revelation, and a human witness at that, and therefore never infallible.

What about this sovereignty of God in relation to the doctrine of election? Barth believes in predestination but not in a predestination of some unto life and a reprobation of others to death, as Calvin did. His idea of predestination is that all as sinners are death doomed, and all in Christ elected to life. Is this universalism? It would seem to be though as a doctrine Barth expressly opposes it. Whether or not he does practically is another question. His own statement is that God "wills that the rejected man should believe, and as a believer should become an elect reprobate."[1] (Incidentally, such a statement is a good example of Barth's method of going

---

[1] *Church Dogmatics,* II, 2, 563.

round and round in order to confront you with the whole truth.)

For Barth, social responsibilities are also governed by the sovereign revelation of God in the resurrected Christ. He believes that a Christian should understand the social movements of his day but shouldn't take too serious an interest in them. Christians are to bear witness, not to their own achievements, but to God's sovereign grace.

This in general is Barth's emphasis and point of view. It is certainly similar to the emphasis of the Reformation, but it is also basically dissimilar. It is certainly not the same as our evangelical faith.

7

Brunner's Point of View— Human Nature

THE VIEWPOINT of Emil Brunner may be said to start with the idea of human nature, for, he says, that will determine our viewpoint concerning civilization around us. To be human is to stand in a certain relationship to God, and that relationship is being in the image of God, which in turn means deriving our being from God. Man is called to obedience to God and is made to live in community with his fellowmen. Thus man is to live in love, and he fulfills that for which he was created to the extent that he loves.

Sin, therefore, is self-centeredness, for that is a contradiction to what God intended for man's life. Self-centeredness, Brunner points out, does not only express itself in a wanton life, but can also find expression in an ascetic life, for withdrawal from the world may be motivated by a desire to protect oneself. However, Brunner denies the doctrine of total depravity, and the account of Adam's sin in Genesis 3 is not historic fact as we understand history. Adam was not a real individual who lived at the beginning of history, but he merely represents man at every stage of his development including the present one. The story of Adam's fall (and it is nothing more than a story) is the story of all of us. As a matter of fact, Brunner is quite glad that science has liberated us from depending on Genesis 3 for the truth concerning man. Of course this means that Genesis is not a true account, and while sin is a fact, it did not originate in the fall of a single man called Adam who lived in a garden called Eden at a certain time in history.

In spite of this, it must be recognized that Brunner attempts to be biblical. However, he does not make as much use of biblical texts as Barth does, but he agrees with Barth in conceiving of the Bible as a witness to revelation only. To quote a verse from the Bible as proof of anything would be inadequate to the neoorthodox mind. However, it is easy to see why this theology has been hailed as the new orthodoxy, for its emphasis on the sinfulness of man was like throwing cold water in the faces of men who had been lulled to sleep by liberalism's rosy view of man's nature, and of course that emphasis on sinfulness is the emphasis of the Bible. These similarities between orthodoxy and neoorthodoxy must not cloud the very basic differences. Sin means sin, but depravity does not mean total depravity; and original sin means nothing if the truth of Genesis 3 is denied.

Because of his view that the conception of man is determinative, Brunner speaks at length about Christian conduct in relation to the state and the economic system. The basic motive for all Christian conduct, he rightly asserts, is the motive of being a forgiven sinner. Christian life is a gift from God, and we live it not as a task but as a gift. His whole idea of the powerlessness of the law to motivate is much to the point. Moreover, he points out, in this life motivated by love there is need for order. It is required in order to restrain evil and in order to express good (e.g., imagine that there were 20,000 cholera victims on the Jericho road instead of the one victim of robbers—organization is obviously needed to express good). In general, the Christian's attitude should be conservative in accepting the existing order, and yet there will be times when Christians must work for a change in that system. But at all times the believer, while abiding in his calling, will work to infuse love into it.

Likewise, Brunner teaches, the state—even the heathen state—is sanctioned by the will of God. The Christian should work for the improvement of whatever kind of government under which he is born. What is the ideal government? Brunner's answer to this question is certainly thought-provoking, for he discusses the merits and demerits of totalitarianism, democracy, and the federated state (of which his native Switzerland is an example). He concludes that the federated state is really the nearest to the ideal form of government.

The economic system is also ordained of God for our well-being, for God himself has set a value on work. What is the best form of economic system? Again his discussion of this question is provocative, but his conclusion is not quite so definite. Capitalism and socialism are both rejected; his ideal will guarantee that the right man would get the right job by means of regulation without state ownership.

The reader should not get the idea that Brunner's writings are only concerned with social orders. We have omitted discussing his view of revelation and the Scriptures, because in this he is in substantial agreement with Barth. We are only trying to point out the differences between the points of view of the two men, and the chief difference is that Brunner pays more attention to the Christian's relationship to the world in which he lives. One might say that he relates sovereignty to social orders, and the connecting link of that relationship is his understanding of human nature. Brunner seems to stand on the middle ground between Barth, who almost disallows much interest in social orders, and Niebuhr, who practically makes it his total system. However, in all other matters Brunner is an orthodox neoorthodox and comes in for the same criticism as others who follow this teaching.

8

Niebuhr's Point of View—Society

THE BACKGROUND of Reinhold Niebuhr has had much to do with the shaping of his theology. He saw liberalism so optimistic as to have little strength. In that Detroit pastorate he saw capitalism so materialistic as to have little Christianity. The foundation of his theology is neoorthodox, but the superstructure is clearly social gospel, and in some ways the superstructure is foundational, for theological concepts are interpreted in the light of social solidarity.

In this view Niebuhr would say that sin was more social than spiritual, and that the evangelistic appeal should be with a view to converting society, not individuals. The Sermon on the Mount should be the law and code for business life today. Niebuhr certainly does not believe in the Reformation doctrine of sin, and yet he attempts to apply the ideas of the doctrine to society. Genesis 3 is a myth, and by this he means truth thrown into the form of a good story. The picture in Genesis 3 is something like the picture on an Easter seal—the crippled child which is shown is stylized as are the other details in the picture, but the picture represents real crippled children who do have a very real need. So Adam and Eve and the Garden of Eden are imaginary, but sin is real and true. This is truth of significance and not truth of fact. Niebuhr is consistent with this idea when he points out that much of the rest of the Bible is cast in this same myth form. The error of such a view is apparent. The Lord Jesus did not believe that Adam and Eve were anything less than real persons (Matt. 19:4-6); but if we believe Niebuhr, then we must believe the Lord was mistaken. Then the question comes, if He were mistaken about this, how can we be sure of anything else He said? Niebuhr should consider that perhaps the Lord was also mistaken about the practicality of the Sermon on the Mount. Maybe Karl Marx had the truth—he did not believe that Genesis 3 was a factual account!

Original sin, therefore, is only a symbol according to this teaching. Man is conscious that he is not what he ought to be, and that is original sin. Adam before the fall merely represents (truth of significance) what was God's intention for human life; after the fall, what human life is in the frustration of that intention.

How does this idea of original sin affect society? This is really Niebuhr's burden. Man, he charges, has either reduced himself to the animal level or tried to elevate himself to the divine level. The first is the sin of sensuality; the second, of pride. Man thinks that science and human advancement will do the same for human beings as it has done for things. On this point Niebuhr's critical analysis is too true and painfully penetrating. He reminds us that Germany was a very advanced nation when it entered World War II. Advancement in good things always brings with it advance in evil. He cites instances where countries will break treaties "in the interests of world peace," and then points to the businessman who will bribe an Oriental ruler and then come home to talk about the "white man's burden."

31

In this, of course, Niebuhr's point is well taken. However, he has missed the point of why these things are so, for his concern about sin is in relation to community or collective life and not in relation to individually depraved human hearts. As long as the fall of man, total depravity, and original sin are rejected as real facts (truths of fact and not merely truths of significance) there can never be any understanding of the problems of society, let alone a solution of them. The pieces of the puzzle of how men can live together can never begin to be solved until men individually know peace with God, and men can only know that through the blood of the Cross of Jesus Christ the Son of God.

How does Niebuhr propose to solve society's problems? The solution is by believing in the resurrection of the body. However, this does not mean physical resurrection; it means social progress. In other words, the body is an integral part of personality, and as such, cannot be repudiated in the interests of spiritual things. Thus when life reaches its ultimate (resurrection—but now, not in the future) it will include the body (social progress now). That is the resurrection of the body!

This social progress is accomplished by a balance of power, love, and justice. Society has to have power groups because it has to be organized, but the Christian is to permeate society with sacrificial love. However, he cannot do that without some qualification, for, for instance, if no Christian resisted evil as the Sermon on the Mount suggests, aggression would break out in its worst forms. The thing that keeps love and power in balance is justice, which is the way love is translated into social action. It should be constantly changing for the better, and the struggle for change must never cease. This is Niebuhr's road to social progress.

There are many strands of truth in Niebuhr's ideas concerning the Christian and society, and it is sometimes difficult to discern the error. God's hope for this world surely does not lie in social regeneration, but in regeneration of individual hearts through faith in the substitutionary death of the Son of God. A child of God thus regenerated is expected to live in the world in certain relations which are specifically defined in the Bible. But he does not live thus with the false hope that such living will bring in a utopian state; rather, his every effort, including all of his social relationships, is bent toward winning men out of the world which he knows to be doomed. Social progress is not an end, though it may be a means, not a means to the end of social utopia, but to the end that God's elect shall be won to a saving faith in Christ.

9

God and Angels

HAVING SURVEYED the particular emphases of the leaders of neoorthodoxy, we now turn to the task of summarizing the teachings of the system under doctrinal categories. These statements must of necessity be general; consequently, what might be true of the system may not be affirmed by every teacher of it.

Neoorthodoxy sees no need to prove the existence of God, for it is assumed throughout the system. Actually, according to their teaching, no man could prove the existence of God. No man can say that *He is,* nor can any church say it. The reason is simple—no statement about God can be made except on the ground that God has already spoken first and manifested Himself to man. When we try to prove He exists, then we are guilty of making God the object. When He says He exists, then God is the subject; and God is wholly the subject and not the object. It is this concept, especially in Barth, of God's being subject and not object that has been called the "wholly other" idea of God.

How does this God reveal Himself? Ultra-neoorthodoxy, if we may coin such a term, says that, although God may use history and experience as media of revelation, the sole revelation of God is in the Christ. More moderate neoorthodoxy says that God also reveals Himself in other ways such as nature. However, in general the teaching is that the principal revelation of God is in the Word, Christ. In Christ God broke into our world of time and space, and the principal era of the revelation of God is the period of the life of Jesus.

One would think from this that the life of Jesus would have a very important place in the teachings of neoorthodoxy. But this is not the case. It should be remembered that neoorthodoxy was a reaction against the liberal's investigations into the "Jesus of history"; thus in the early days of neoorthodoxy Barth even went so far as to assign no value to Jesus of Nazareth. He even spoke of Him as inferior in certain respects to St. Francis of Assisi.[1] In another place he says: "Jesus Christ in fact is also the Rabbi of Nazareth, historically so difficult to get information about, and when it is got, one whose activity is so easily a little commonplace alongside more than one other founder of a religion and even alongside many later representatives of his own 'religion.' "[2] Of course, this is consistent with Barthianism's acceptance of the critics' attacks on the historicity of the Gospels. If you believe that many of the stories in the Gospels were concocted by the Early Church, or that John's Gospel is a novel about Jesus written by a trembling old man, then you have to search for some other significance for the Christ.

What, then, is the significance of Jesus Christ? Logically it cannot be in His life, if the records of that life are not trustworthy; rather, they say it lies in His Cross. The Cross is the revelation of God that all things in this world are vain and doomed to extinction. The Cross is

[1] *The Epistle to the Romans,* p. 57.
[2] *Church Dogmatics,* I, 1, 188.

also (here comes the dialectic) the sign of the election of all in Christ to life. The Cross is at once a symbol both of despair and hope.

Concerning the Holy Spirit, neoorthodoxy has very little to say. When what little there is, is boiled down, it amounts to the fact that the Spirit of God is not considered to be a Person of the Trinity but only a mode of expression of God. He is merely identified with certain aspects of the work of God and of Christ. One could hardly expect a higher concept when John's Gospel, the great treatise on the Holy Spirit, is little more than the fictitious product of an imagination.

It is a little difficult to tell whether Barthians believe in the existence of angels as objective beings. They are called "ontological functionaries possessing half-divine powers"—whatever that means. Actually, they are not thought of as having objective existence because, we are told, angels are to be understood entirely from the point of view of their service, not their being, and their service is strictly *God's* action upon men. That pretty well denies their real substantial existence.

Demons and the Devil seem to be even farther down the scale of reality, for, we are told, we cannot believe in them in the way we may believe in God or even the angels. They are "the myth of all mythologies."[3] They are only lies, but not lies that can be ignored, because they do have power! (Here is another good example of going round and round until you are supposedly confronted with the truth as a whole.)

In all of this it is evident that everything revolves around God and His revelation in Christ; and yet that revelation is not primarily in the life or sayings of Jesus

---

[3] *Ibid.*, III, 3, 611.

but in the Cross. Everything is made subservient to this idea; thus the Holy Spirit is just a particular mode of the working of God, and angels, the Devil, and demons are denied substantial existence. Everything is bent around the emphasis of the revelation of God in the Word, Christ.

10

Man and Salvation

BARTHIANISM takes a very serious view of the limitations of man. He is finite, he is a dependent creature, he is insufficient, and yet he is a creature of infinite possibilities which can only be fully realized in eternity. Man is akin to nature, for he shares many things with the animals, but he is also open to a higher world of the spirit, for he has powers which the animals do not possess. And yet it is recognized that even these higher faculties cannot save man, for there are basic problems in man which no psychoanalysis, however accurate, or education, however thorough, or science, however advanced, can deal with. These basic problems are called sin.

Can we define the Barthian concept of sin more precisely? In general, sin is the mistake of making ourselves the center of things instead of God. We can do this in many ways, but it amounts to the same thing. However, the important thing for the reader to know is that this concept of sin is not a deduction from the biblical text; rather, it is based on a concept concerning anxiety which the philosopher Kierkegaard had. This is not to say that Barthians do not use biblical texts in their discussions about sin; but the Bible is treated as having only relative, not absolute, authority. And yet even on such a

38

basis sin is seen to be exceeding sinful in its work in man. Man is said to be hopeless, standing on the very brink of Hell, and too much a sinner even to recognize himself as such. This is one of those inconsistencies of Barthianism—evangelical-like statements based on a modernistic view of the Bible. This is why the movement was hailed as a new orthodoxy when in reality it is a false orthodoxy.

The concept of sin and the concept of salvation go dialectically arm in arm in neoorthodoxy. The great gulf which sin has fixed between God and man cannot be bridged except God does it. Religion gets some harsh treatment in Barthianism because it is man's effort to climb up to God—something which is absolutely impossible to do, and of course that is true. Salvation has to be the work of God in man, for sin can never be overcome by human goodness. How does this come about? First, man despairs; out of this, contrition is born; out of this faith is conceived; and in faith is newness of life and power.[1] Salvation is the shattering or breaking of self, and this may come in a single crisis experience or in repeated ones.

But how does the Cross figure in this scheme of salvation? Jesus Christ is a Saviour in that He is a revealer, and that seems to be the main point of His work on Calvary. He reveals the fact that God takes upon Himself man's sin, and that assurance is enough for our reconciliation. This is not to minimize the importance that Barthians place on the Cross. Reconciliation, propitiation, substitution are all included in their discussions, and many statements are sound. For instance, Barth says: "What takes place in the Crucifixion of Christ is

---

[1] Niebuhr, *The Nature and Destiny of Man,* II, 61.

that God's Son takes to Himself that which must come to the creature existing in revolt . . . He makes the misery of His creature His own. To what end? So that His creature may go out freely, so that the burden which it has laid upon itself may be borne, borne away."[2]

Alone, a statement like this is hard to criticize, but to praise it would be to make the mistake of isolating it from the entire system. With all of its good emphasis on the Cross, the trumpet of Barthianism still gives at best an uncertain sound about substitutionary atonement. It is true that Barth insists that whatever theory of the atonement one holds, it must pay attention to the fact that it was "for us,"[3] but his explanation of what "for us" means is hardly that the sinless Saviour died in my place and for my sins. He says: *"For us*—that is, insofar as by His death we recognize the law of our own dying; insofar as in His death the invisible God becomes *for us* visible; insofar as His death is the place where atonement with God takes place . . . and where we, who have rejected our Creator, return to His love; and insofar as in His death the paradox of the righteousness and the identity of His holy wrath and His forgiving mercy becomes *for us*—the Truth."[4]

This is why we say that the main point in Barthianism of the work of Christ on the cross seems to be that of revealing and assuring. It is especially significant that the Barthian emphasis is on the cross of Christ and never on the blood of Christ. The testimony of the Bible is clear and strong on this point (I John 1:7), but the testimony of neoorthodoxy is vague and weak.

We have noted before in the doctrine of original sin

---

[2] *Dogmatics in Outline,* p. 116.
[3] *Loc. cit.*
[4] *The Epistle to the Romans,* p. 160.

that the facts of the case seem to make little difference to Barthian doctrines. The same is true of the doctrine of the resurrection. What actually happened at the tomb is of minor consequence to the doctrine of resurrection. Whether or not you actually believe in the physical, bodily resurrection of the Lord Jesus matters little; the point is that in resurrection the opposition between man and God is finally overcome. The Cross showed that opposition as nothing else can; the resurrection finally removed it, for the resurrection is an event of reversal. But what is a doctrine of resurrection without a fact of resurrection? What does resurrection mean if the Lord is still in the tomb? What difference does it make what the Early Church preached if it was all based on a lie? The whole idea is meaningless without a literal, bodily, factual, historical resurrection.

It has already been suggested that there is a suspicion of universalism in Barthianism. It comes from the doctrine of election which is a denial of the Calvinistic doctrine (they call it a restatement!), for in Christ all are elected to life.

This then is their idea of salvation. It sometimes seems to come very near the point but never hits it. Some Barthians believe that Jesus was a sinner which, of course, would nullify the whole biblical concept of salvation. At best its statements are fuzzy. Doctrinally, the concept lacks many essentials and cannot be called orthodox; practically, it may contain enough truth to bring salvation to some—only God knows.

11

The Church and Future Things

THE DOCTRINE OF THE CHURCH in neoorthodoxy is presented in relation to two main emphases: the one relates it to the Bible; the other, to the State. We have already spoken of the first and will speak of it again later, but, in a word, the Word of God reaches us through the intermediary of the Scriptures, and the Scriptures come to us sustained by the life of the Church. The authority of the Church, however, is always under the Word, but it is nevertheless a very real authority. We must come to the Bible knowing the interpretations that the Church has already made concerning it. We should know the contents of the Confessions and the interpretations of the Church history though we are not bound by them.

It should be said to the credit of Barthians that their knowledge of Church history is usually very excellent. Fundamentalists are often too eager to dismiss such knowledge as an intruder on one's own personal relation to the Bible, but such an attitude is neither intellectual nor spiritual. The Barthian dictum that one should come under the discipline of the knowledge of Church history before exercising his own judgment is a good one.

With the exception of Barth himself one of the chief emphases among the group concerns the relation of Church and State. The State is sanctioned by God, and it is all-important that there be a continuity of order in the world. Even if there is a change in the government, it is essential that the change be effected quickly so there is no break in governmental functions. The Christian should always be working toward the ideal, for this work of purifying the State is the work of bringing in the kingdom of God. The Church should support any political instrument which may arise to keep order and to make that order a just one. Barthians by their own example allow for anything from a very conservative attitude toward reform movements to a very radical approach to social ethics.

In the realm of individual ethics neoorthodoxy also speaks. A couple of examples in this area will suffice. Marriage, for instance, is looked upon as a very serious and holy matter. When a couple is joined together by God then there can be no divorce. However, it is admitted that sometimes the marriage was not consummated by God, and divorce, though never good, may be necessary. Remarriage, at least according to Barth's viewpoint, is not allowed. Concerning war, Barth is for the most part a neutralist. He does see occasions when the State may have to defend itself within its own borders, but in general he thinks the practices of Ghandi came nearer the biblical pattern for defense.

We have heard a great deal in recent years about the second coming of Christ because of the World Council of Churches. It has been said that the European theologians because of Barthian influence believed in it, and that American theologians because of liberal influences did not. As a general statement this is true enough because neoorthodoxy seems to believe in a return of Christ which will be an actual event that ends time. And yet Brunner says: "It is equally indisputable that the statements of the Bible concerning the future are not only to some extent contradictory, but are laden with mythological ideas which have become alien and partly even meaningless to us."[1] The idea of a kingdom in Revelation 20 is said to be a "plainly fantastic theory." Here again we find neoorthodoxy holding to a doctrine of the second coming of Christ but not particularly concerned with the scriptural facts about it. Perhaps it would be more accurate to say that Barthians take the idea of the second coming very seriously but not very literally (and I mean literal according to the picture painted by the facts of the Bible). Liberals do not take it seriously.

There is a very serious view, too, in Barthianism of judgment. However, in the thought of Christ's being the Judge is not primarily the idea of One who rewards some and punishes others; the main point is that the Judge will restore order. For the Christian the result of judgment will be freedom from the conception of evil which has plagued him all through history. What about Hell? Moderate neoorthodoxy says that we must discard all literalistic concepts of the everlasting fires of Hell, but that we should keep the testimony of the heart which affirms the fear of judgment. In other words, keep the reality of it without the truth of it—the doctrine without the facts.

Of future things, then, we are again forced to the conclusion that although there is a very serious outlook on this doctrine, it is an outlook which is void of the literal facts of the biblical teaching about the future. One grows very weary of saying, "Neoorthodoxy believes, but . . ." The serious outlook brands it as neoorthodoxy; the lack of factual basis, as pseudoorthodoxy.

---

[1] *Eternal Hope,* p. 26.

12

The Bible

IT SHOULD BE APPARENT by now that one of the chief differences between orthodoxy and neoorthodoxy relates to the Bible. It concerns a basic attitude toward the Bible which affects and colors the entire doctrinal system. When one is tempted to glorify neoorthodoxy for its specific statements or its usefulness historically, he should consider and reconsider what it has to say about the Scriptures.

In the first place, Barthians align themselves with the liberal school of biblical criticism. They hold to the Wellhausen theory, they believe that the last part of Isaiah was written after the exile, they frankly say that the accounts of the resurrection of Christ are conflicting, that the Gospel of John is not a historical account, and that the Pastoral Epistles were not written by Paul. We should thank the critics, they say, for their work, for through them we have gained a fuller understanding of the message of the Bible. Brunner blatantly proclaims: "Orthodoxy has become impossible for anyone who knows anything of science. This I would call fortunate."[1] And yet evangelicals are lulled into thinking that this is a new orthodoxy. (It could be called new if you under-

---

[1] *The Word and the World,* p. 38.

stand new to mean opposed to the old.) The damage
that liberalism has done to the Bible can never be esti-
mated, and this is the side neoorthodoxy takes.

We have already observed that Barthianism believes
that revelation is primarily in Jesus Christ. The Bible, so
to speak, is on the periphery of the circle of revelation,
and Jesus Christ is the center of that circle. The Word
is Jesus Christ; the Bible is a witness to the Word. It is
a word about the Word. Some parts of the Bible are better words about the Word than other parts, but all
of .it is merely a witness to the Word, Christ. One
Barthian puts it this way: "If there is anything to which
the name of 'rediscovery' may be applied, it is surely to
this view of the Bible (which is but the Bible's view of
itself) as *witness* to the Word of God. It liberates us
from the false antithesis which had been set up by 'orthodoxy' and 'liberalism,' through each concentrating its
attention on one aspect of the Bible, to the detriment of
the other, and enables us to see it in both its aspects,
without detriment of either."[2]

Is the Bible the Word of God, then? Yes and no (to
use a good Barthian dialectic). Barthians can say that
it is in the sense that it is a word about the Word; indeed, Karl Barth has said that he would be willing to
speak of the Bible on the shelf as the Word of God. but
beyond any doubt the more general Barthian view and
the more correct one (the standard of correctness being
agreement on the meaning of all the words used in the
statement) is that the Bible becomes the Word of God.
There is no quality in the Bible itself that can be used
to prove that it is the Word of God, they say. That certainly means that it cannot be the Word of God but can

---

[2] G. Hendry, "The Rediscovery of the Bible," *Reformation Old
and New,* p. 144.

only become so when it overpowers us and gains the mastery over us.[3]

What, then, of inspiration? One of the most intellectually dishonest tricks of Barthianism is to set up a fundamentalist straw-man theory of inspiration and then proceed to tear it apart and replace it with their superior theory. Barthians charge evangelicals with holding to the dictation theory of inspiration. They say that we believe that the human writers of the Scripture were passive instruments like a typewriter on which God typed His message. "This view," one of them writes, "issued in the notorious doctrine of verbal infallibility, which lay for so long like a blight upon the Protestant Church. It is the great and undisputed merit of modern criticism that it demolished this doctrine and rediscovered the human character of the Bible."[4] This is not intellectually fair or honest; orthodoxy does not hold to a dictation view of inspiration.[5] Nevertheless, this is the straw man which neoorthodoxy huffs and puffs against. What is the Barthian view, then? The same writer states it quite plainly. "When the Word of God creates faith in us, this is God's own work, His miracle, His in-Spirit-ing. It is not in our power to make it happen. At the best we can pray for it. This, in all its simplicity, is the doctrine of the inspiration of the Bible."[6]

In explaining the meaning of II Timothy 3:14-17 and II Peter 1:21, Barth says that the important thing

---

[3] *Church Dogmatics*, I, 2, 561.

[4] Hendry, *op. cit.*, p. 145.

[5] See Machen, *Christianity and Liberalism*, pp. 73-74, for a clear denial from a conservative of the dictation theory of inspiration. Why don't Barthians read this (or other such statements by conservatives) before making their fantastic statements about what evangelicals believe?

[6] Hendry, *op. cit.*, p. 152, based on *Church Dogmatics*, I, 2, 590.

47

in both passages is that in neither is there any occasion to think that the authors had special experiences. Inspiration, he says, is to be understood as "the act of revelation in which the prophets and apostles in their humanity become what they were, and in which alone they in their humanity can also become for us what they are."[7] This of course means that the text is a human product full of errors, but that when God uses it to overpower us, it becomes His Word.

Can a Bible like this have any authority? Oh, yes, they say. Its authority is the encounter of faith with the Christ of Scripture. It is an instrument which points to Christ and thus has instrumental, not inherent, authority. Some parts are more authoritative than others because they are better pointers to Christ. But, one wonders, how can any of it be worth much when it is so full of errors, which is the only conclusion we can come to if we accept, as neoorthodoxy does, the "findings" of criticism?

This is a brief sketch of the neoorthodox view of the Bible. We have purposely tried to avoid going too far afield into the criticism of it at this point but have merely tried to list the salient ideas. To sum up: their doctrine includes orthodox terminology built on liberal exegesis; it attempts to have inspiration without infallibility and authority without actuality. What kind of a Bible is that?

---

[7] *Church Dogmatics,* I, 2, 563.

13

Criticism I

EVERY SYSTEM of theology likes to think it is the most logical and consistent of all, and neoorthodoxy is no exception. Actually, Barthianism is most inconsistent and illogical, and this is the first major area of criticism of the system.

It is not only the evangelicals who have pointed out the intellectual inconsistency of neoorthodoxy, but also the liberals. Of course, the liberals do not object at all to neoorthodoxy's use of the results of destructive criticism, but they attack the Barthians on the ground that for all practical purposes they do not use those results to arrive at their conclusions, for if they did they could not possibly be Barthians but would have to be liberals. If you hold to the results of criticism then, you cannot even talk evangelically, thus, the liberals charge, when the Barthians try to do both, they are acting most illogically. For instance, if John's Gospel is not historical fact, as neoorthodoxy holds, then how can you speak at all about our Lord's being the Bread of Life? Or, to reverse the question, how can you believe in Christ as the Bread of Life without believing in a historical basis to John's Gospel?

Barthianism tries to hold to the truth of what John

says and at the same time hold that the Gospel is fictitious. One liberal puts it this way: Barthians hold "that these doctrines have some important element of truth in them but are not true in the form in which they were traditionally accepted, while any attempt to say what *is* true in them ends in logical incoherence."[1]

Conservatives cannot help but agree with this charge of inconsistency brought by the liberals against the Barthians. It is both illogical and impossible to accept the "findings" of destructive criticism and preach and speak in orthodox terms. There is no question but that neoorthodoxy is an attempt—and an unsuccessful one at that—to reinterpret traditional Christianity in such a way as to make it more acceptable to the so-called intellectual advance of the age. In the eyes of Barthians fundamentalism is a sacrifice of the intellect, while their own system is respectable to the mind and evangelical to the ears. One is inclined to agree with another liberal who calls this a very strange state of mind.[2]

Nowhere is this inconsistency more clearly evident than in the Barthian idea of history and its relation to Adam and Christ. Barth's concept of history is that it is divided into two kinds—history which is historiographical, and history which is not. Historiographical means that it may be understood from a creaturely context. The account of creation, for instance, is not historiographical because it was the act of God by which the creature became a creature. Therefore, the account of creation cannot be expressed in creaturely terms and is unhistoriographical history. Brunner uses the term "primal history" to describe all history that is on the plane of faith—creation, the fall, salvation, and glorifica-

1 *Religious Liberals Reply,* p. 19.
2 *Ibid.,* p. 4.

tion. This term denotes a real occurrence which is related to our world of time and space but which does not lie within it. Other writers resort to the phrase "true myth" to describe the events of creation and the fall. But whatever term is used, it boils down to the fact that these events did not actually happen within our world of time and space.

Thus the Genesis account of creation and the fall is rejected as history—as most of us understand history. Science, the Barthians say, has delivered us from having to believe the Genesis stories, and through this scientific deliverance we are supposed to be able to see the real meaning of the accounts. In other words, to take the fall as an example, that event did not actually happen at a certain time to two real people in an actual garden, but the story merely expresses the dimension of sin in that I am Adam and you are Adam. The reader can easily see how such a view can enable the Barthian to preach sin and yet hold to all the liberal ideas about the origin of Genesis.

But how is this particular example about Adam inconsistent? It is inconsistent in three ways: first, Barthians are inconsistent in their popular presentation of this doctrine. Writing popularly they are forced to speak of the fall of Adam as though it really were history. Their sleight-of-hand tricks with the meaning of history simply cannot be comprehended by the average person; hence this resorting to the usual historical presentation of the story. This use of orthodox terminology especially for popular consumption is what makes neoorthodoxy not only a pseudoorthodoxy but a very dangerous one at that.

Second, this example is inconsistent theologically. The great theological doctrine, which is based on the Genesis account of the fall, is the doctrine of the imputation of the sin of Adam to the race (Rom. 5:12-21). The old New England Primer was correct when it explained the letter *A* in the alphabet by the phrase, "In Adam's fall we sinned all." The point Paul is making in the Romans passage is simply that as sin was imputed to the race in Adam, so also righteousness is imputed to the believer in Christ. If the one imputation is not real (because it is not based on the same kind of history as the other), then how do I have any logical right to say that the other imputation is real? Of course, if the Barthian does not hold to the imputation of the righteousness of Christ, then he is right back to the liberal position. And if he does hold it, then he must either also hold to the imputation of Adam's sin or be illogical. Neoorthodoxy utterly abandons the parallelism in Romans 5:12-21 because it refuses to understand the fall as a historical occurrence within our world of time and space.

The third inconsistency of this example concerns the practical thought of the Romans passage. Paul's teaching clearly is that at a certain time, in a certain place, a certain person, Adam, did a certain thing. If you remove the time-space idea from the passage, what is left? You can continue to call the story true myth, or unhistoriographical history, or primal history, or whatever you will, but "the prosaic mind can hardly escape the suspicion that an event which did not happen in time and space, did not happen at all."[3]

Thus, in its doctrine of history, Barthianism is inconsistent with itself, illogical in its principles, and impractical in its presentation. God did not speak about the fall of man in terms hard to understand. Yet if we depended on neoorthodoxy one wonders if we would

[3] Jewett, *Emil Brunner's Concept of Revelation,* p. 148.

actually know with certainty anything about the fall, and one is afraid that we would be terribly confused finding that out.

Let us look at another example of the outworking of this neoorthodox idea of history—this time in the case of the life of Christ. If anything is on the plane of faith in the Barthian system, certainly this is, and therefore the entire life of Christ should be primal history and not related to the world of time and space. This would be logical, but the Word became flesh, and that means a relationship to the world of time and space. Thus the life of Christ which is on the faith plane ought not belong to historiographical history, but it obviously does. How does neoorthodoxy solve this dilemma? It is done by saying that the facts of the life of Christ are immaterial to faith. Actually, they say, the Gospels are written from the standpoint of faith and for faith and they do not intend to report simply what happened. Theoretically, this is a fairly logical answer, but neoorthodoxy does not put this answer into practice; for, having said that faith does not need facts, they proceed to talk about and appeal to certain facts in the life of Christ. The Sermon on the Mount and the Lord's Supper are both used, to mention but two. To appeal to any of these facts about Christ's life is a practical repudiation of the principle that the Gospels were written for faith and not for facts, and to admit that faith in Christ needs historical facts about Christ is to deny their doctrine of history. Either way they are caught in illogical inconsistency.

If the Gospels were written from the viewpoint of faith, and if the writers described Christ through the eyes of faith and not through the eyes of historians, then it becomes easy to say, as neoorthodoxy does, that not one word that John puts into the mouth of the Lord was actually spoken. It becomes easy to accept all the findings of liberalism about the Gospels. But neoorthodoxy is unwilling to go to the liberals' conclusion about the Gospels, and insists that we retain the truths of the Gospels even though we cannot believe the record. The events did not happen the way the writers reported them, but the truths are still supposed to have enough basis in something to be true. For instance, it does not matter what actually happened at the tomb; the important thing is that we can believe in resurrection. But if I do not know the facts of what did happen at the tomb, how can I define my concept of resurrection?

Furthermore, was Peter not wearing glasses of faith when he talked, after the resurrection and after Pentecost, about the resurrection of Jesus of Nazareth as an historiographical fact to which there were many competent witnesses (Acts 2:32; 10:38-41)? If he were mistaken, then he and the Early Church were preaching lies. If he was not mistaken, then it does make a difference what happened at the tomb, and the facts of the life of Christ have to be true as reported for genuine faith.

Thus, in the matter of the life of Christ, neoorthodoxy is inconsistent and illogical. By admitting facts about Christ, their concept of history is repudiated. What they do admit about the life of Christ is altered and colored by the results of higher criticism which they accept but which they inconsistently refuse to preach to a logical end. The critical approach to the Gospels is modified or synthesized into the neoorthodox system by their attempt to preach the orthodox truths while building on the liberal approach to the facts. Actually, it is impossible to make such a synthesis. To be consistent neoorthodoxy would either have to be thoroughly liberal or thoroughly conservative. Either the Lord Jesus is all that the writers say He is, every detail of the Gospel records being true, or He is what the liberals say He is, and Christianity is either a fraud or a great mistake. He cannot be what the liberals say He is and at the same time what the conservatives believe He is. That is inconsistent, illogical, and impossible. And that is exactly the neoorthodox position.

14

Criticism II

NEOORTHODOXY has been trumpeted as a biblical theology which has returned to Reformation principles. In spite of these claims, however, it cannot be called orthodoxy but has to be entitled a new orthodoxy; thus, there must be some differences between Reformation theology and Barthianism. In these differences lies the second area of criticism.

The chief characteristic of the theology of the Reformation was its return to the Bible as the final authority in all matters.[1] The chief characteristic of neoorthodoxy is its call to the Word of God as the authority, but the Word of God is not synonymous with the Bible, and this is the point of deception.

It has already been pointed out that the Word of God, according to the neoorthodox conception, is particularly the revelational event of Jesus Christ. The authority of such a Word is then the encounter of faith with that Christ. It is true that Christ is seen in the Bible and that God addresses the individual in the Bible, but the Bible is merely a witness to the revelation of the Word. The witness, or the Bible, is of course human and fallible; yet, in spite of this, it can point to infallible truth.

---

[1] Schaff, *History of the Christian Church,* VI, 16-17 (1895 ed.) .

This truth is the Word of God, but it is not necessarily the Bible; and this Bible of ours is full of errors and only possesses instrumental authority. This is a far cry from the Reformation doctrine of the absolute authority of an infallible Book. Thus, plainly our criticism of neo-orthodoxy in the realm of bibliology centers around the two ideas of inspiration and authority.

Verbal inspiration does not mean that God handed the Bible—especially the King James Version—to man already bound in gilt-edged India paper. Neither does it mean that the human authors of the various books of the Bible were merely stenographers to whom God dictated His message. It does mean that God directed (not dictated to) the human authors, using their own styles and interests, bearing them along by the Holy Spirit so that His message was accurately recorded in the original manuscripts. Since we do not possess any of the original manuscripts, this means that conservatives are interested in any investigation that will determine the most accurate text.

Textual criticism is a very exact and skilled science, the recent results of which bear out the fact that the Hebrew and Greek texts which we do possess are accurate to a very high degree. Our doctrine of verbal inspiration also means that, having determined what the text is (not the meaning of it), it is infallibly accurate, and that means that every word, including singulars and plurals and tenses, is as God desired it to be.

Neoorthodoxy does not employ textual criticism merely to determine the construction of the original text (which is legitimate), but it also uses destructive criticism to determine the meaning of the text. For instance, if textual criticism affirms, which it does, that the word *Paul* is part of I Timothy 1:1, II Timothy 1:1, and

Titus 1:1 then that settles for me the question of the authorship of the Pastorals. Paul wrote them. But destructive criticism says that other considerations lead to the conclusion that there are too many differences in style for the Pastorals to be Paul's work. Anyone who holds verbal inspiration cannot accept this conclusion, but neoorthodoxy can because it does not accept verbal inspiration and does accept destructive criticism. In other words, conservatives believe that the Bible is itself an infallible revelation while neoorthodoxy says that it is only a fallible witness to revelation.

Let us put it another way. Barthianism says that we do not have to hold to verbal inspiration because a distinction is to be made between revelation and the human witness to revelation. The Bible is the record of the latter and need not, then, be inspired. Can such a distinction be maintained? For several reasons we must answer no.

Such a distinction, which makes the Bible mere witness, is highly artificial. Another's illustration of this artificiality is the best there is, and it is briefly this.[2] Barthians would have to admit that when Peter said, "Thou art the Christ," his confession was inspired because that was clearly a revelation of God to him. Now, the question is, if Barthians will admit inspiration of the direct statement "Thou art the Christ," what right do they have to limit a sovereign God (and they talk so much about sovereignty) in His ability to inspire a man to report indirectly that He is the Christ? The whole thing is artificial, for God is certainly able to guard and guide the pen of Peter or Paul or any other biblical writer as carefully as the lips of Peter. It is impossible to make a distinction between the human witness to the

[2] Jewett, *op. cit.,* pp. 161-64.

truth (the Bible) and the truth itself. The witness is the truth. Barthians should face the possibility that if God be God, and if one statement in the Bible can be inerrantly inspired, then the whole Bible can be.

A second reason why you cannot say that the Bible is merely a witness to the truth, and therefore not inspired, is the use the Lord Jesus made of the Bible. Obviously, any appeal to the Bible as final authority would mean that the Bible is inspired. That is just the reason why neoorthodoxy tries to maintain this distinction between the Bible and the Word. Not to maintain it would lead to a doctrine of verbal inspiration. But what did the Lord do? He appealed again and again to the Bible as the final authority which could never be broken. He quoted the Old Testament in His temptation, and His answer to Satan was simply put on the basis that "it is written" not "it witnesses." (Cf. Matt. 4:4, 7, 10; 19:3-9 and Gen. 2:24; John 10:35.) The belief of our Lord was that the Bible is the Word of God which is inspired and authoritative. Christ, the revelation of God, also revealed clearly what God thinks of His Bible.

Thus neoorthodoxy finds itself on the horns of a dilemma. If it repudiates the verbally inspired authoritative external standard of the Bible, the result will either be liberalism, with its deemphasis of the Bible, or mysticism with its denial of an external standard. If it accepts verbal inspiration, the result is orthodoxy and a denial of the higher criticism which it has embraced.

The neoorthodox idea of authority is as unacceptable as that of inspiration. The need for authority is readily recognized, but the kind of authority which Barthianism assigns to the Bible is instrumental authority. It is an instrument to point to the revelation of Christ and has authority as an instrument. Some parts of the instrument, they admit, are better than others; thus all parts of the Bible are not equally authoritative even in this instrumental sense. There are at least five points of criticism of such an idea of authority.

First, this concept of authority carries with it the idea of errantry of the Scriptures. This has been pointed out above.

Second, it leads to double talk about the validity of even the witness value of the Bible. The resurrection will serve as a good example. Barthians say that the accounts of the resurrection in the Bible are not the ground of our faith in the resurrection; nevertheless, they are an important element in the witness to revelation of the resurrection, and this revelation is the ground for our faith. Reduced to simple double talk this means that theoretically we would not need the Bible accounts of the resurrection in order to believe in it, but admittedly they help, and actually we could not believe without them.

Third, it reduces the authority of the Bible to the same level as the authority inherent in the preaching of the Church. The New Testament is simply the preaching of the apostolic Church which may have a historical priority—but nothing else—because the preaching of the Church today is also the voice of God. Therefore, how can the preaching of the first century, which is recorded in the Bible, have any more authority than our preaching today?

Fourth, this concept of authority opens the door for other witnesses to the revelation of God outside the Bible. It seems that Barthians are aware of this possibility but dismiss any contenders with the Bible as bad witnesses. But who is to judge? Perhaps the Koran is a better witness to revelation, and it could well be without contradicting the Barthian concept of the authority of the Bible.

Fifth, it actually reduces the authority of the Bible to a subjective vanishing point. There is really no authority except what you or I or any individual is willing to assign to the Bible. Perhaps no other point in the system illustrates better the statement that "neoorthodoxy is a state of mind." They want authority without an external standard; they want the Word without the Bible. Is this Reformation doctrine? It is the farthest removed from it. Is this a new orthodoxy? It is a deceivingly false orthodoxy.

15

Conclusion

NEOORTHODOXY is a theological hoax. It attempts to
preserve the message of the Bible while denying the
facts of the Bible. It speaks of important and real truths
about God, sin, man, and the Cross. But, because of
neoorthodoxy's acceptance of the liberal view of the
Scriptures, the truths are based on nothing more than
good stories, which may contain a grain of truth, but
which also are greatly embellished. Original sin is the
truest thing in the world, but the account of it in
Genesis is only a story. The resurrection of Christ is
the truest thing in the world, but the Gospel accounts
of it are "hopelessly garbled." Christ is the Bread of
Life, but of course, not one word of the Gospel of John
is historical. Is it too strong a statement to say that
neoorthodoxy is a theological hoax?

Attention has been called in this survey of neoorthodoxy to the various emphases of its leading exponents,
to the main tenets of its theology, and to some basic
crticisms of its system. Although Barthianism's avowed
purpose was to create a synthesis above and beyond the
liberal-orthodox antitheses, it has scarcely succeeded in
doing little more than creating an illogical system which
sometimes leans to consistent liberalism and even sometimes to consistent orthodoxy, but the system is more

like an unbalanced pendulum than a synthesis. Of course, the neoorthodox answer to this usually is, "They don't understand our position." But such recourse to a sort of gnostic intellectualism does not obliterate the illogical foundational principles of the system, and if one accepts those principles, he has lost the orthodox message of the Bible—not stepped higher to find it.

We have also tried to show that neoorthodoxy is unbiblical and thus dissimilar to Reformation theology. The Reformation brought men back to the Bible as the authority in doctrine and practice; the so-called new reformation does *not* call men back to the Bible as the basic, objective, and final authority. In the final analysis the authority of neoorthodoxy vanishes into subjectivism.

One fears, too, that neoorthodoxy often breeds a false sense of security and satisfaction among its own adherents, for they think they have found a way to think intellectually and preach evangelically. The student in the university and the layman in the pew can both be fed satisfactorily on neoorthodoxy. This seems like the perfect synthesis; yet one knows from experience that neoorthodoxy is divisive when it permeates evangelical circles, and it is under sharp criticism from liberal circles. In other words, it cannot get along because of its doctrinal position with either group, and this is as it should be. Let it also be a warning to Barthian and conservative alike of the true nature of this teaching.

This is the Barthian system. More often than not neoorthodox practice is inconsistent with the system in coming closer to conservatives' preaching rather than that of the liberals. Herein lies the greatest danger of deception, for this breeds among evangelicals a dangerous tolerance of Barthianism. Conservatives become so interested in the fact that men are being called back to the Word and even to the Bible that they forget what the Word means in neoorthodoxy and what kind of a Bible the Barthians have. Evangelicals must never forget that neoorthodoxy has just as openly taken its stand against what it considers the errors of conservatism as it has against the errors of liberalism. It is just as sure that conservatives have misconstrued the Bible as it is that the liberals have. It is not neoorthodoxy but pseudo-orthodoxy.

May God give us discernment of the issues at stake, clear understanding of the truth, wholehearted committal to the authority of the Bible, God's Word, and deep conviction of heart to speak the truth in love.